TSP MILLIONAIRE 2020

Are you on the right track towards becoming a TSP millionaire? If you answered "No", you came to the right place. If you said "Yes", great, I invite you to compare your strategy to mine. It doesn't require in-depth knowledge on how the stock market works. You don't need to conduct research, watch financial news, or study market trends. Instead, just like succeeding in the military, you need to be disciplined and resilient. This guide will teach you: my perspective on long term investing, specific advice on which funds to invest in and how much to contribute, behavioral investing, eliminating procrastination, fear, and feeling vulnerable, along with investment and withdrawal strategies. This information is especially for anyone that needs help setting up their TSP, isn't completely confident in their strategy, or is not currently contributing. Even if you have a good understanding of the stock market and the TSP, this information will change the way you think about investing.

The TSP is one of the best retirement accounts in the country, mostly because it has very inexpensive management fees. However, there are some potential mistakes TSP investors can make, and pitfalls that everyone needs to be aware of. Most of the official TSP information that I received in my military career has come in the form of presentations about TSP facts and fund characteristics. The information was overwhelming and did not provide any specific advice to help make a decision regarding TSP contributions and asset allocation. There are also very few books on the market about the TSP. These books cover every detail of the TSP, essentially regurgitating the information you can find at TSP.gov. They do not provide specific advice on how to structure your TSP. For a new investor that is not familiar with how the stock market works, the information can be complicated and intimidating. This guide leaves out the basic information that you can easily find on TSP.gov, and gets right to the information that you need to know.

The overwhelming information on the TSP website often leaves service members confused about investing in the TSP. As a result, they often give up or become fearful, and contribute a small amount only into the G fund, or nothing at all. When you ask for specific advice that is right for you, representatives will direct you to seek assistance from a professional financial advisor. Financial advisors will charge you a fee for that advice. As a financial advisor that is also one of your fellow service members that wants you to retire successfully, I am giving you the advice for free. I became a licensed financial advisor in New York back in 2001, and I enjoy coaching service members on how to structure and allocate funds in their TSP. Most importantly, I coach service members on behavioral finance and investing. I try to spread this advice to all service members and federal employees that have an open mind and are willing to listen. I am on a mission to help people make a plan to have the right amount of income in retirement. If you don't have that plan, then you are on the wrong track. Investing in the TSP should be simple, the plan is not complicated, and the most important part of the plan is to not change it. Take charge and don't neglect it. After all, the TSP is a cornerstone of your overall retirement plan, along with a possible pension, social security income, and any other retirement accounts you contribute to.

In order to graduate high school, we had to pass algebra and pre-calculus. Learning how stocks, bonds, and mutual funds work, probably wasn't part of the curriculum. To be as brief as possible, here is a quick class on stock, bonds, mutual funds, and indexes: Corporate stock is a share of a company and a corporate bond is a loan to a company. So, buying a stock means purchasing a share of the company, and becoming a part owner. Buying a bond means loaning funds to a company that is promising to pay it back over a certain length of time, plus interest.

A mutual fund is a collection of stocks, grouped together in a package. Think of a stock as a wooden pencil, it can easily break or snap in half, just like a single corporation can fail or go bankrupt. Think of a mutual fund as a hundred pencils together in one group, clutched in your hands, with thick rubber bands wrapped around it. It won't snap or get broken in half. That is the power of the mutual fund, if one of the stocks in the fund fails, it can easily be removed and replaced with a different stock by the fund manager. Therefore, mutual funds can be less volatile and risky than individual stocks, and they can deliver impressive gains in the long term.

Stock indexes measure the stock market or subsets of stocks, such as small cap (smaller companies) or large cap stocks (larger companies). For instance the S&P 500 index, is a measurement of the 500 best stocks of large companies in the USA. The C fund in the TSP is based on the S&P 500. So, the C, S, I, and F funds that you can choose to invest in with the TSP, are all similar to index funds, because they track certain indexes and seek to match the returns of those indexes. However, to be accurate, these 4 TSP funds are not actual index funds. They are funds managed by Blackrock Capital Advisors, and they seek to replicate the indexes. In other words, privately managed funds that replicate indexes by containing all the same stocks or bonds as the ones listed in each of the indexes.

The G fund is a collection of U.S. Treasury notes and bonds. The F fund is a collection of government bonds, corporate bonds, and mortgage backed securities based on the Barclays Capital Aggregate Bond Index. The C, S, and I funds are based on stock indexes. Again, the C fund is a collection of large cap common stocks, based on the S&P 500 index, which is the best 500 companies in the stock market. The

"S" fund is a collection of small cap (smaller companies) stocks, based on the Dow Jones U.S. Completion Total Stock Market Index. This index consists of all other U.S. company stocks that are not listed on the S&P 500. Do not get that index confused with the Dow Jones Industrial Average, which is 30 stocks, tracked and reported on a daily basis in the financial media, they are two different indexes. The "I" fund (international stocks) is based on the Morgan Stanley Capital International EAFE (Europe, Australasia, Far East) Index.

What have you been taught about the TSP fund choices? You may have been told that the G fund is the most conservative and guaranteed not to lose value, and therefore carries the least risk. You may have been told the F fund is safer than the C, S, and I stock funds. Most investors think that stock funds are the riskiest. You have probably heard stories from friends, family, or coworkers saying things like: "I know someone who had all of his savings in the C fund and lost a bunch of money a few years back". *That's not actually how it happened. All of these assumptions are completely incorrect.*

Risk in terms of investing for retirement, is the chance **that you may fail to reach your goal**. Putting all of your money in the G fund may sound like a good idea because its "safe" and guaranteed not to lose money. Investors that fear volatility only contribute to the G fund. However, when we factor in inflation, the increase in prices and decrease in value of the dollar over time, you *can* lose money. This risk is called inflation risk. So, **the G fund carries the most risk** towards not meeting your financial goals.

The F fund is a collection of bonds. Investing in a bond, is loaning money to a company at a set interest rate. Then, the business pays off the loan and enjoys the profits from their expansion. The lender just gets their loaned money back plus interest. Investing in bonds is basically investing in debt. Percentage gains from investing in bonds are low compared to stock funds in the long term. The average return of the C fund over any 10 year period is always a multiple of the lower F fund average returns, sometimes 2x, 3x, or 4x, as you can see from the bottom line of the upcoming chart. In the last 40 years, the price of a stamp has more than tripled due to inflation, meanwhile the interest rates offered on government and corporate bonds has decreased. Therefore when investing for the long term, stock funds are the safest, while bond funds and CDs are the riskiest.

We don't know anyone that took a huge loss *while in the C fund*. While the market was down, these investors panicked, lost discipline and resiliency, and emotions lead them to make an irrational decision. They sold out of the C fund at a loss, instead of staying in and buying more. Investors often make that mistake when they do not have a financial advisor to talk them out of it. Take a look at how the C fund has recently performed, chart from TSP.gov:

Individual Funds Annual Returns (10 Yr Summary)

Year	G Fund	F Fund	C Fund	S Fund	I Fund
2008	3.75%	5.45%	(36.99%)	(38.32%)	(42.43%)
2009	2.97%	5.99%	26.68%	34.85%	30.04%
2010	2.81%	6.71%	15.06%	29.06%	7.94%
2011	2.45%	7.89%	2.11%	(3.38%)	(11.81%)
2012	1.47%	4.29%	16.07%	18.57%	18.62%
2013	1.89%	(1.68%)	32.45%	38.35%	22.13%
2014	2.31%	6.73%	13.78%	7.80%	(5.27%)
2015	2.04%	0.91%	1.46%	(2.92%)	(0.51%)
2016	1.82%	2.91%	12.01%	16.35%	2.10%
2017	2.33%	3.82%	21.82%	18.22%	25.42%
10 Yr Compound	2.38%	4.27%	8.55%	9.37%	2.23%

Percentages in ( ) are negative.

This isn't the newest chart available on the TSP website, but I prefer to show this version because it lists 2008. Take a look at 2008 on the chart, the C fund decreased 36.99%, many worried investors decided to cut their losses and move in to the G fund, where they have still never recovered. The common investor sees their investments declining, gets spooked by negative financial media reports, doesn't have a financial advisor coaching him, and so he jumps ship, selling out of the investment at a huge loss. Instead of surrendering, if he just stayed in the C fund, he would have been buying more at low prices (dollar cost averaging), while the fund value bounced back up 26.68% in 2009, and 15.06% in 2010. As always, the fund made a full recovery. Then look at 2012-2014, you can see my point, in total, the C fund is up 250% since then. The C fund is based on our nation's greatest companies, and as patriotic Americans, we benefit financially by supporting our economy, and investing in these great companies as the best long term plan to generate wealth and combat rising inflation.

Lifecycle "L" funds allocate your investment in all 5 funds and adjust the allocation percentages for lower volatility as you near your target date. What is your target date, maybe 2040 or 2050? Most people assume that is when they retire or when they start making withdrawals. Either way, as you get closer to that target date, the L funds move most of your assets into the G funds, which contradicts the financial advice I am providing. Even if you are retiring in 5 years from now, that does not mean that you need to move most of your assets to the G fund. Your retirement could last around 30 or 40 years. For example, if you move all of your savings to the G fund when you turn 60, your savings will no longer grow with the stock market while you are in your withdrawal phase. That could put you in an increased risk of potentially outliving your savings. The best situation to use target date funds is outside of the TSP, in a college savings plan. That is because there is a more accurate date when the funds will be needed, which is when the child reaches age 18. Then, you may have a 4 year window when the child is attending school. That short timeline is when you need all of the funds and want to protect the savings from volatility.

Volatility of stock funds does not equal risk, and a short-term decrease in value is not risk, as long as you don't sell the investment. Owning stock funds for the long term has consistently been the best investment you can make. Even outside of the TSP, there are many mutual funds with solid long term track records, averaging annual returns of around 10-12%. These funds can seem volatile and unpredictable at times. However, they are intended as long term investments, and when you look at the average annual percentage gains of these funds, you realize that no other investment can compare.

Historically, every time the stock market has taken a nose dive it has never taken long to make a full recovery. Watching fear mongering financial news reports is what leads the average investor to jump ship at the worst possible time. The key is having the discipline to hold on and not to sell out of the funds. Even if they are declining rapidly, discipline and patience will prevail. Before you read this guide, you may have felt that investing in the C fund would make you vulnerable to losing your savings. Fear of the negative financial media can be overwhelming. You don't have to fear the stock market, because being aware of your own behavior makes you a successful investor. One of the keys to successful long-term investing is remaining optimistic while the market is down. During these times, purchase more shares to lower your cost basis.

In order to be a successful equity investor, you must be disciplined and resilient. The stock market experiences *average 15% temporary decline every year*, and an average *30% temporary decline every 5 years*. You have to be willing to endure that, to be a successful investor. The best way to ensure you achieve your financial goals is to resist the temptation to trade in and out of funds and don't change your plan. No one can consistently time the market, it is impossible.

Remember, it is natural and normal for the stock market to decline. It increases and decreases every year. As I am writing this in March 2020, the S&P 500 has recently decreased by 34% due to the COVID-19 pandemic, and it's possible that it declines further. However, in terms of temporary market declines, this time is not different than other big declines. Declines are always temporary and present a fantastic opportunity to increase contributions and purchase more shares at low prices. Think of it as going to the grocery store, and buying items that are on sale.

The best time to start or increase TSP contributions is now! You can implement this plan to become a TSP millionaire by contributing as much as you can to your TSP every month. Even if you are unable to part with a large percentage of your paycheck, don't dismiss this advice. Increasing your contributions may feel slightly uncomfortable at first, but you just need to do it, you will thank me later. If you are a drilling reservist, try contributing the maximum percentage of your monthly drill pay allowed on the MyPay website. Increase your TSP contribution percentage, live with it for a month, then adjust accordingly if needed. Be disciplined, and once you find a contribution percentage that you can live with, don't decrease it! Also, don't take out TSP loans, this is your retirement funding, don't make the mistake of using it for anything else or deviate from the plan. If you need money, try to obtain it from somewhere else.

Whether you should contribute to a Traditional (before tax) or a Roth TSP (after tax), depends on your anticipated future tax situation. If you anticipate that you will be in a higher tax bracket during retirement, choose Roth. Hint: If you are a member of the active duty military, choose Roth. If you are unsure of whether your tax bracket in retirement will be higher or lower than it is now, you can also contribute to both. The type of account that you choose isn't really as important as it may seem, when compared to the importance of the investment strategy and sticking to the plan. As long as you are cognizant of your behavior, and you stay disciplined and resilient while contributing as much as you can, you will be fine.

	C Fund*	S&P 500 Index
1-Year	31.45%	31.49%
3-Year	15.25%	15.27%
5-Year	11.71%	11.70%
10-Year	13.59%	13.56%
Since January 29, 1988	10.66%	10.67%

*After expenses

The above charts show performance of the C fund since its inception in 1988, courtesy of TSP.gov. The chart shows that the C fund, despite the high rate of volatility, has averaged over 10% return annually since 1988. That means on average, the C fund increases 10% per year. 10% average annual return is great. Remember the stock market is the best investment that you can make to combat inflation. Investors don't lose money while *in* the stock market, only when they sell at a loss. The stock market always rises in the long term. In fact, the average annual return for the S&P 500 since 1926 to 2020, is also 10%!

For example, when you are a TSP millionaire, you can hypothetically withdraw 5-10% of your TSP every year ($50-$100k) and still maintain your account balance above $1 million due to potential average annual returns of 8-10%. Therefore, you are only withdrawing the interest, and can still leave the remaining account balance to your beneficiary upon death. Of course, the plan is not to just reach an account balance of $1M, but to surpass it. That way your annual 5-10% withdrawals can be much higher than $50-100k. That is the definition of financial independence, no longer having to work, and living off interest and dividends from your investments. If you move all of your funding to the G fund for that false sense of safety as most people do, you could dwindle your account balance down to $0 from your withdrawals, and outlive your TSP savings, while leaving nothing for your family.

In 1978, the price of a stamp was 15 cents. In 2018, the price increased to 50 cents. So, in 40 years, the price of a stamp has more than tripled. What if you start withdrawing from your TSP at age 60? You might live until 100, that's also 40 years. If you have all of your money in the G fund at 60, the interest rate you are earning may keep up with the rate of inflation, or might not, either way, your account balance will steadily decrease as you make withdrawals, until you reach $0. You might reach $0 before you make it to 80 years, maybe even before you make it to 70 years. Again, if you have your savings in the C fund, you could hypothetically withdraw 5 -10% of your balance every year while averaging an 8-10% increase every year and still remain a millionaire.

As shown on the chart, **compound interest makes your savings grow exponentially.** This is similar to a snowball effect, the account will look small in the first few years of consistent investing, but after that it will start snowballing. Keep in mind that past performance is not indicative of future results. The purpose of this chart is to help you visualize how compounding heavily contributes to your wealth accumulation. $100 invested 30 years ago in the C fund is worth $2,533, in 2020. Use the TSP calculator on www.tsp.gov.called "How Much Will My Savings Grow". Here's a basic example: If you are 25 years old, making $40,000 annually, and contributed 20% of your paycheck for 15 years, with an average return of 10%, you would be a TSP millionaire by around age 50. You would have $4 million by age 65. Even if you are already 40 or 50 years old, it is not too late to start. Plug your info into the calculator, look at some of the potential results for yourself, make a plan, and stick to it!

I am advising you to invest in stock mutual funds now and through your retirement. Here is my advice: **allocate your TSP contributions in the C fund 100%.** If you want to diversify amongst the other stock funds, try C, S, I funds, 60%, 20%, 20%, or 80%, 10%, 10%. To maximize your long term investment gains you won't need the F, G, or L funds.

Take advantage of the contribution matching. If you are a civilian employee in the Federal Employee

Retirement System (FERS) or a service member in the Blended Retirement System (BRS), the government will match up to 5% of your contribution. It seems like a lot of service members are under the impression that if they just contribute the minimum to receive the match, then that's good enough. But it's not. To make the most of your TSP in retirement you may need to contribute 10-20% of your base pay. Again, reference the calculator on TSP.gov called "How Much Will My Savings Grow".

Even if you can only invest the minimum to receive the match, you should still prioritize that over paying extra on debts. Even if you are paying off a loan at 20% interest, it doesn't compare to the match that you are receiving from the government. Think of the matching contribution as the government paying you 100% interest.

Do not attempt to profit by actively trading in and out of your TSP funds. This is a long term plan, contribute to the plan and leave it alone, try not to look at it. A study at one of the major brokerage firms was conducted a few years back to see which of their investment accounts performed the best. It turned out the winners were clients that forgot they had an account. Your TSP account is similar to a bar of soap, the more you touch it, the smaller it gets. Attempting to time the market is something that no one can do consistently, and leads to selling low and buying high, which will lead to diminished returns in the long term.

It's like skipping the grocery store when they are having a sale, then deciding to go shopping right after the sales are over. The last 10 years have been the best stock market run in history, there are a lot TSP websites out there claiming that they can trade in and out their TSP funds and beat the "buy and hold" strategy, and if they do, it is not by much. It's not consistent, and also very time consuming and stressful. Huge institutional investors like Warren Buffet don't attempt to time the market, so why should we? The best strategy is to pick a fund allocation and stick with it, no matter what. This guide is helping you to create a plan that can't fail, as long as you don't fail the plan.

The TSP and an IRA are different accounts. The **TSP (Thrift Savings Plan)** is the federal employee retirement account, similar to the 401k plan that a corporation would offer its employees. The TSP is an employer sponsored account provided by the federal government. As of 2020, the maximum contribution is $19,500 per year, and additional $6,500 if you are over 50 years old, called a "catch up" contribution. If you are in the BRS or the civilian FERS system, the government will match up to 5% of your contributions. For more information on details of contribution matching, there are charts with that info on the BRS and FERS respective websites. If you are serving in a combat zone, your tax free income can go right into the Roth TSP so you won't have to ever pay taxes on it. The contribution amounts change often, but as of 2020, if you are serving in a combat zone you can contribute $57,000 per calendar year.

An **IRA is an Individual Retirement Account**, which is a separate account that you can contribute to outside of the TSP. You can open an IRA account with most banks and brokerage firms. As of 2020, the maximum annual IRA contribution is $6,000, or $7,000 if you are over 50 years old. Again, that extra $1,000 is called a "catch up" contribution. The earliest you should begin to withdraw from TSP and IRA accounts without possibly incurring a 10% penalty from the IRS, is age 59 ½. **Think of both of these types of accounts as legal IRS tax loopholes that you should be taking advantage of**, that's why the IRS has set limits on the annual contributions. You should not be investing in other types of accounts if you have not first taken advantage of the TSP and IRA. If you are already investing both accounts and still have extra funds to invest, that's when you should start looking into variable annuities. Therefore, the top 3 investment priorities in order, are TSP, IRA, variable annuity. You should not be investing in individual investment accounts outside of these 3 types of accounts, unless you still have extra funds after participating heavily in all 3.

You should contribute to a Roth IRA to help with diversification. The TSP is by far the best retirement plan available in the USA mostly because it has very low sales charges, but it only offers 3 stock mutual fund choices. Meanwhile, there are over 8,000 mutual funds you can invest in outside of the TSP. Diversify with other mutual funds in an IRA instead of limiting yourself to the 3 stock funds in the TSP.

In closing, try to minimize your debt and maximize your TSP and IRA contributions as much as possible. Invest in the C fund. The S and I funds are ok, too. Use the calculator on the TSP website to visualize your plan, stay motivated towards your goals, and don't change the plan. Remain disciplined and resilient, and don't let the news media scare you in to making an irrational decision. Don't let anything lead you astray from the sure path to your long term financial goals. Call me anytime, and ask me anything, I am glad to help.

Important Tips:

1) Rebalancing your TSP - As you accumulate value in the TSP funds and the values of the funds fluctuate, you will notice that your asset allocation will grow eschewed. Another benefit of the TSP is that rebalancing between funds is not a taxable event. However, automatic rebalancing is only available in the L funds. Therefore, I recommend that you do a manual or "hard" quarterly or annual rebalance between the C, S, and I funds to keep the allocation at, for example, 60%, 20%, and 20%. You can complete a hard rebalance by first signing into your TSP account and clicking "Account Balance". Then, look at the "Account Distribution" table and see if it has changed considerably from your desired asset allocation. If so, just click "Interfund Transfers" on the left pane and simply enter the desired percentages of each fund then click submit. It is a tedious process, and a bit archaic to do a hard rebalance every quarter or year, but until the TSP offers automatic rebalancing, we will need to do it this way. What we are doing is essentially grabbing some of the gains from the funds that have gotten more expensive, and redistributing that money to the funds that are cheaper. Rebalancing is important because it can increase your annual returns by around 1%. If you do it annually, try to do it sometime in January – March.

2) As you near retirement, move 2 years' worth of your required income to the G fund as an emergency

fund. That way, if you need to make a withdrawal, and the C, S, and I fund values are down, you can withdraw from the G fund while waiting for the stock funds to recover. Also, if you are nearing retirement and this advice makes sense to you, but you are unsure how exactly to proceed with your TSP in retirement, send me a message and I can help you make a specific plan.

3) Is your SGLI or FEGLI benefit sufficient for your family? If you ever purchase additional insurance, make sure that the policy has a war clause for service members. Do you have a will and trust set up? Have you ever really looked at your car insurance? Take a look at your policy. Is it something like $50,000 to cover damage and injuries? That's not enough. You might be able to increase it without paying too much more per month. Don't leave yourself vulnerable like that. You don't want to have you finances crushed because you didn't have adequate car insurance in the event of an accident.

4) Have you ever been approached by a financial advisors pushing highly complex investments called indexed universal life insurance policies? I won't name any names, but if it ever happens to you, run for the hills. These are advisors working for multi-level marketing companies. You can spot them because they spend way more time recruiting than they do trying obtain clients. These products are doomed to fail and become too expensive to maintain later in life.

The result will be forfeiting the policy due to inability to pay the extremely high premiums.

5) Mutual funds are an investment, real estate is a job. It can be tough for an active duty service member to potentially purchase a second home and maybe even have to manage it from long distance after a move. Finding the right tenant, having to deal with repairs, sometimes at odd hours of the night. It is expensive to buy and sell, and expensive to manage. The C fund doesn't come with a utility bills or a leaky roof. Also, would you want to own part of the building that Google works in, or part of the actual company?

6) If you are into buying small amounts of stock on the side, through the various smartphone apps available these days, that's fine. However, just don't categorize that as part of your retirement plan. Think of those stock purchasing apps as expendable casino money, you need to be ok with the fact that you could lose every dollar that you invested.

7) How much do I need for retirement? A lot of math involved to be accurate, but here is a simple way to come up with a general estimate based off what you earn currently. Subtract what you will receive from social security, you can find that amount by using a retirement calculator ssa.gov. Multiply by 20 years then use a compound interest calculator to account for inflation by adding 3% for every year until you retire.

8) Keep track of your TSP account login and password. If you lose it, you have to request TSP to mail your login information to the home address that they have on file. Sometimes that address is not updated. Either way, it's a huge inconvenience. I have many friends and colleagues that asked me for advice on how to set up their TSP, and when I am ready to help them, they can't login. Remember that the MyPay site is where you input the percentage of pay that you want to contribute, but TSP.gov is where you input the fund allocation. Sometimes a month goes by before they receive their information in the mail and are able to finally login, especially soldiers overseas that have an outdated address on their account.

About me: I am an Active Duty Army Warrant Officer and a licensed financial advisor. I provide retirement planning services and help people invest in stocks, bonds, mutual funds, annuities, 401(k)s, IRAs, 529 college savings plans, etc. So, my clients trust me to manage millions of dollars in their investment accounts, and the Army trusts me to manage millions of dollars' worth of equipment.

I am an independent financial advisor, meaning that I can provide products from many different companies as opposed to just one. The difference between me and the other companies is that I build long term relationships with a smaller group of clients that I am able to provide more attention to, and when my clients need me they can just call me directly. When you work with discount brokerages, you talk to random advisors on the phone that either don't know how to help you, or do not have a vested interest in your financial success. I am doing this because I believe military service members and federal employees deserve better service than that. I can work with you on the way in, as well as on the way out, when you are retired and taking your income distributions.

I am not like other advisors because this is not my primary job. I don't sell investment products to make a living. I just do it because I truly enjoy teaching people about long term investing and like to help my friends, soldiers, and their families. Therefore, I do not upsell my clients or push expensive products. Service members trust me because I wear the uniform and I know the system. I have been building a book of business consisting of clients that are mostly military, enlisted and officers, that respect me, trust me, and are in it for the long term. I don't charge by the hour so feel free to take advantage and email me at james.patrick.lamb@gmail.com and ask me anything, I am proud to help.